A souvenir guide

North Devon Coast and Countryside

Tor McIntosh

Above Holden Head, Exmoor

Welcome to
North Devon

The wild and beautiful North Devon coast and countryside is a gateway to the great outdoors. It's a place you can visit all year round to feel the wind on your face, smell the salty sea air and taste a delicious Devonshire cream tea.

With its surf-pounded beaches, isolated bracken-covered heathlands, deep-cut wooded combes with tumbling rivers and waterfalls, and dramatic coastline of towering cliffs, craggy headlands and secretive coves, you will discover a varied landscape that is rich in history and home to an abundance of wildlife.

The diversity of this stunning stretch of coastline means it has something to offer anyone looking to enjoy some time in the outdoors: from intrepid explorers keen to run, kayak, stand-up paddleboard or paraglide along the coastline, to slow adventurers who prefer to unhurriedly explore the area.

The National Trust is proud to be the custodian of 50 miles of this vast stretch of coastline, which lies in the nationally protected North Devon Coast Area of Outstanding Natural Beauty (AONB), is part of a national park and includes a number of designated Sites of Special Scientific Interest (SSSI) and Special Areas of Conservation (SAC). It is our responsibility and privilege to protect this stunning coastline so that it can be enjoyed, explored and experienced today and far into the future.

Left Cows grazing on Woolacombe Warren

The History of North Devon

Signs of early human activity are embedded in North Devon's landscape, with remains of bracken-covered earthworks and numerous discoveries of prehistoric artefacts dating as far back as the Middle Stone Age.

Prehistoric activity

Over 7,000 years ago, when sea levels were much lower, Baggy Point – the promontory between Croyde and Woolacombe – stood as a hill above a vast coastal plain. Surrounded by bountiful hunting and fishing grounds, it attracted Mesolithic (c.6000–4000BC) hunter-gatherers to what archaeologists believe was a seasonal encampment. Evidence of this early human activity was first discovered in 1865, when flint tools and waste from tool production were excavated, along with fragments of Neolithic (c.4000–2500BC) pottery – a telltale sign that the land was not only being used for hunting, but for living in too. Over the past 150 years, large quantities of prehistoric artefacts have been unearthed across Baggy Point dating back to the Middle Stone Age (Mesolithic) through to the Bronze Age (c.2500–700BC).

By the Bronze Age there had been a transformation from nomadic hunter-gatherers to permanent farming communities. On remote, cliff-top locations small settlements were built and hilltops were commandeered for ceremonial purposes. Traces of Bronze Age inhabitation are strewn across the region. Fine examples are visible in West Exmoor, where earthwork remains of hut circles can be seen on the north-east slopes of Holdstone Down, while nearby lies a series of bracken-covered round barrows and cairns (circular tombs) in various states of disrepair. In 2009 a Second World War aerial survey of Little Hangman emerged that revealed prehistoric earthworks encircling its summit. These are believed to be tor enclosures dating back to the late Neolithic or early Bronze Age.

Late Prehistoric to Saxon

As the name implies, the Iron Age (c.700BC–AD43) saw the introduction of iron workings, but more significant to the landscape was the development of fortified enclosures on hilltops, reflecting the emergence of tribal kingdoms and the need for security in a more divided society. North Devon's high sea cliffs and headlands, with their commanding views along the coastline and across the Bristol Channel, offered perfect territory for such hill forts. Promontory forts at Windbury Head and Embury Beacon – located on the coastlines either side of Hartland Point – are impressive examples of Iron Age settlements built over 2,500 years ago, but due to their cliff-top positions large sections have slowly been lost to cliff erosion. Annual scrub clearance and careful management of these sites by the National Trust allows visitors to see and appreciate what is left of these Scheduled Ancient Monuments.

The landscape of West Exmoor reveals more evidence of Iron Age human activity, as well as traces of Roman occupation. On the steep wooded slopes of the East Lyn Valley lie two hill top enclosures, known as Myrtleberry North and South Camps. Not much evidence remains today – you need a trained eye to identify the remnants of hut platforms, ditches and ramparts – but from their elevated positions the earthwork defences of Countisbury Castle, on the summit of Wind Hill, are clearly visible on the opposite side of the valley. The strategic position of this promontory fort overlooking the Bristol Channel has led some archaeologists to believe it was the site of the Battle of Arx Cynuit in AD878, where an outnumbered Anglo-Saxon army miraculously defeated the invading Vikings, changing the course of English history.

The remains of Martinhoe Castle, a Roman fortlet that consisted of a signal station and beacon, is tactically sited on the cliff-top above Heddon's Mouth. With clear views across the Bristol Channel to South Wales it was manned by a century of soldiers for a short period between AD55 and AD75 to keep watch for possible attacks from the Silures tribe in South Wales. Excavations in the early 1960s unearthed ramparts, along with Roman artefacts, including pottery and coins from the reign of Emperor Nero.

Left The landscape around the former Windbury Hillfort

Shipwrecks and smugglers

With 62 miles (100km) of coastline, stretching from the Cornish to the Somerset borders, North Devon has a rich heritage of maritime activity.

Before the arrival of road and rail transport large numbers of vessels voyaged along the coast to and from the Bristol Channel ports, while ships were used to transport goods, both legally and illegally, in to and out of the area.

The Sailors' Grave

Over the centuries countless ships have met their demise along the wild North Devon coast with many lives lost, leading to its nickname: 'The Sailors' Grave'.

A combination of elements contributed to the overwhelming number of shipwrecks, including inclement weather, poor visibility, dangerous currents and an unforgiving rocky shoreline. The local geology showed no mercy to ships that strayed ashore, with submerged jagged reefs and saw-toothed rocks ready to snag unsuspecting vessels.

From the late 1600s to 1899 there were over 200 shipwrecks recorded along the coastline. In Morte Bay alone, 50 vessels were wrecked or stranded between 1816 and 1918 and more than half met their tragic end on the jagged rocky outcrop of Morte Point with its deadly Morte Stone, separated by a deep channel from the Point and perilously hidden on the incoming tide. Legend has it that Grunta Beach near Morte Point is humorously named after a ship was wrecked and its cargo of pigs escaped ashore.

The remains of most wrecks lie on the seabed, providing plenty of interest for local divers, although remnants from *SS Collier*, a steamship that ran aground between Bull Point and Morte Point on 28 January 1914, can be seen at Rockham beach. All seven members of the crew were rescued, along with the ship's dog, cat and goldfinch, but the ship was beyond repair; at low tide parts of her boiler can be seen, and large metal chain rings are moulded into the rocks.

One of the most tragic shipwrecks was *HMS Weazle*, a 14-gun naval sloop that sank off Baggy Point in February 1799 in a severe gale, drowning all 106 on board. Today one of her cannons is on display outside Mortehoe Museum.

By 1900 three lighthouses were in operation along the coast, with a further two at either end of Lundy Island aiding navigation in the Bristol Channel and significantly reducing the number of shipwrecks along the North Devon coast.

Above George Morland (1763–1804), *The Smugglers*, 1792, oil painting on canvas

Right The remains of the *SS Collier*, wrecked in Rockham Bay in January 1914 on its journey from Milford to Avonmouth

The wreckers

Shipwrecks encouraged the sinister practice of wrecking by locals from the village of Mortehoe. These notorious 'Mortemen' used lanterns to lure ships to dangerous rocks. As the sailors struggled ashore from their wrecked vessels they were brutally clubbed to death or drowned; the law stated that if nobody was left alive after a wreck the local community could claim the cargo. One notorious wrecker was Elizabeth Berry, who would gruesomely drown sailors by holding them underwater with a pitchfork.

The smugglers

With its secluded beaches and hidden coves, the rugged North Devon coast was perfect territory for smugglers. Brandy, wine, gin, salt, tobacco, tea and, rather oddly, playing cards are some of the illicit goods smuggled into the region by these so-called Gentlemen of the Night during the late 18th and early 19th century. Small boats carrying limestone to isolated lime kilns along the coast would contain contraband – collected from French vessels in the Bristol Channel – secreted beneath the stones ready to be received by gangs of smugglers once landed.

The full story of smuggling in North Devon will never be fully known, as much of the trade took place undetected, or the captured boats were taken to South Wales and so not recorded in local Customs books. However, the popularity of smuggling in the south west has left a lasting legacy: the South West Coast Path. Coastguards tirelessly patrolling the cliffs looking for smugglers inadvertently created the 630-mile (1,010-kilometre) footpath around the whole south west peninsula – a route used by many exploring North Devon's coastline today.

Thomas Benson

North Devon's most infamous smuggler was Thomas Benson, a local merchant trader who became MP for Barnstaple in 1747. Despite his high office he was the mastermind behind an elaborate tobacco-smuggling scheme from Lundy Island using convicts that the government believed he had shipped abroad; instead they worked as slaves and were kept in a cave at the south of the island, which today bears Benson's name.

North Devon's industrial heritage

Scattered across this coastal landscape are traces of North Devon's industrial past, when the region relied heavily on lime burning, silver mining and herring fishing.

Lime kilns

In coves all along the North Devon coast you'll discover ruined lime kilns. These old stone buildings are relics of a 19th-century industry that supplied quicklime fertiliser to counter the acidity of Devon's soil. The burnt lime was also used to create building mortar.

Records reveal that kilns were being used as early as the 17th century, but it wasn't until the 1800s that the burning of lime in vast quantities became a significant industry. Local quarries at Combe Martin supplied some of the limestone, but large amounts were also shipped from South Wales, resulting in the majority of kilns being built on beaches or near harbours; the inland lime kilns near Watersmeet House and the elevated kiln near The Torrs in Ilfracombe are all very unusual, although both were served by their own limestone quarries.

By the late 19th century the use of artificial fertilisers, and cement in the building trade, rendered the laborious process of burning lime obsolete. Over 100 years have passed since North Devon's lime kilns were last fired up, and today they stand as monuments to the industrial era.

transportation of the mined metal. Adits and shafts were created above Wild Pear Beach and at Girt Down and West Challacombe to mine both iron and manganese, while varying degrees of success were had mining silver-lead at Old Combmartin and Knap Down mines. Over the centuries these mines were worked and abandoned on numerous occasions by different companies, all trying out the newest technology in a bid to go deeper and further than previous attempts.

Today the only obvious sign of the area's mining past is an ivy-clad stack at Knap Down, the remains of the engine-house at Knap Down Mine, the last successful silver-lead mine, which ceased operating in 1868.

Silver darlings

For centuries the enormous shoals of herring – affectionately known as 'silver darlings' – that appeared in the Bristol Channel each autumn supported a thriving fishing industry. During the 18th century a number of fishing fleets worked out of the small villages and hamlets of Bucks Mills, Clovelly, Lynmouth and Peppercombe, but the harsh weather conditions and fluctuating catches made it a difficult way to make a living. Records show that for six years in the 1740s fishing quotas were worryingly low, impacting on the livelihood of locals. But equally, a glut of fish in 1801 left fishermen virtually giving away cartloads of herring, mackerel, shellfish and whiting for as little as a shilling, to be used as manure. Yet it wasn't the unpredictability of the herring shoals that devastated the trade – it was the First World War. With so many young men never returning from the trenches in Europe, North Devon's fishing industry started to decline. Today the rocky foreshores along North Devon's coastline are perfect habitats for crabs and lobster, resulting in a thriving shellfish industry, with fisheries at Bideford, Clovelly and Ilfracombe supplying shellfish to the wider region.

Above left This cave was once part of the Combe Martin silver mines

Above right Jack Draper, Corney and a friend at Knaps Quarry

Below left The decaying Knap Down engine house in the 1970s; the engine was originally erected by the Combe Down & North Devon mining company in 1843

Silver rush

Before it transformed into the popular seaside resort it is today, Combe Martin (p. 18) was a dirty and industrial mining town thanks to the discovery of silver deep within its cliffs. The earliest recorded extraction of silver ore dates back to 1292 and in 1293, the eldest daughter of King Edward I, Eleanor, had a dowry of 270lbs (122kg) of Combe Martin silver for her marriage to the Duke of Kent. However, it's possible the precious metal was mined during Roman times.

Manganese, iron, lead and copper were also mined in the area. By the late 18th century the fortunes and population of Combe Martin had risen dramatically and its harbour allowed easy

Tourism

The North Devon coast has been a popular tourist spot for over 200 years, enticing Romantic poets seeking inspiration from the breathtaking scenery, along with seaside day-trippers and early surfers with wooden boards. Yet today it still manages to feel 'undiscovered'.

Early visitors

The rugged coastline of North Devon started attracting visitors in the 1790s, when key figures from the new Romantic Movement, including Coleridge, Shelley and Wordsworth, were drawn to the unspoilt, dramatic landscape of Lynmouth. At the time the region was not easily accessible and many of these early visitors were both wealthy and hardy enough to cope with the expensive and arduous journey by horse-drawn cart along ill-kempt roads.

The 19th century

The roads began to improve in the early 17th century, but it was the advent of paddle steamers in the 1820s, carrying early Victorian tourists from Wales and Bristol, that boosted the fortunes of coastal resorts, in particular Ilfracombe and Lynmouth – although a lack of a suitable pier at Lynmouth meant passengers were tediously ferried ashore in small boats.

By the 1850s horse-drawn coach services were transporting visitors to popular haunts, such as the unusual landforms at Valley of Rocks and (with an extra pair of horses at the front) up the exceptionally steep gradient of Countisbury Hill

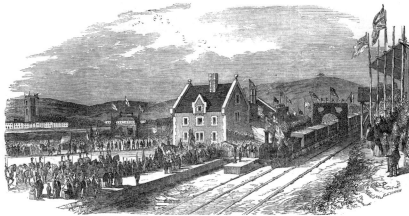

OPENING OF THE NORTH DEVON RAILWAY.—ARRIVAL OF THE TRAIN AT BARNSTAPLE.

NORTH DEVON RAILWAY.

The opening of a further portion of this Railway will, doubtless, be fully appreciated by tourists in search of the picturesque, during the present season. The line follows the valley of the Taw, and will be of the greatest value to a large agricultural district, both for the conveyance of manures and farm produce; at the same time it will open to the tourist an easy access to the delightful scenery of Linton, Ilfracombe, Instow, Clovelly, and the whole of the north coast.

HIGH-STREET, BARNSTAPLE.

TRIUMPHAL ARCH, BARNSTAPLE-BRIDGE.

THE IRON RAILWAY BRIDGE, OVER THE RIVER TAW, NEAR BARNSTAPLE.

Opposite The *Illustrated London News* highlights the opening of the North Devon Railway on 29 July 1854. It shows the arrival of the train at Barnstaple (top), High Street Barnstaple (left centre); triumphal arch, Barnstaple Bridge (right centre); and the iron railway bridge over the River Taw, near Barnstaple (bottom)

Above A group of tourists in Lynmouth, 1911

Right Passengers disembarking at Lynmouth in the early 1900s

Seaside day-trippers

The arrival of the railway line between Exeter and Barnstaple in 1854 opened North Devon up to both trade and tourism, with the latter further boosted with the opening of branch lines to Ilfracombe in 1874 (this now defunct line forms part of the Tarka Trail, a traffic-free cycle path) and Lynton in 1898. The Ilfracombe branch line brought a new type of holidaymaker to North Devon: the seaside day-tripper. With an option to disembark at Mortehoe & Woolacombe station this was the fastest way for town and city dwellers to reach the beach; unfortunately the station was located 600 feet (180 metres) above sea level and two miles (3.2km) from the beach. Nevertheless, in the early 1900s up to 17 trains ran along the line every weekday during the summer months, bringing hordes of day-trippers to the seaside resort of Woolacombe. In 1911, a day return from Exeter would set you back five shillings.

By 1919 Woolacombe's vast white-sand beach was regularly packed with tea tents, beach huts and bathing machines (enclosed wooden carts that sat in the sea and allowed people to change into swimwear out of sight) and the first surfers, wearing woollen bathing suits, were braving the Atlantic waves with wooden boards.

to Exmoor's open moorland. The East Lyn Valley attracted Victorian fern collectors from around the world.

In the early 1900s, the preferred modes of transport were motorcars and charabancs – early buses that were usually open-topped and typically used for leisure trips. By 1920 they had replaced all horse-drawn services and further increased the number of visitors to the area, benefitting local businesses such as the tea-room at Watersmeet House (see p. 28).

It was Lynmouth's success as a tourist destination during the mid-to-late 19th century that inspired extravagant, but ultimately unsuccessful, plans to develop Woody Bay in the 1880s (p. 23) and, the following decade, Holdstone Down (see p. 20) in to holiday resorts. The peace and tranquility of these remote locations today makes you breathe a sigh of relief that such large-scale projects never came to fruition.

Passengers disembarking at Lynmouth

Wartime history

Both World Wars impacted on the people who lived in North Devon, but it was the arrival of US troops near the end of the Second World War that changed the physical fabric of the area and left a lasting legacy.

Many young men from North Devon were enlisted to fight in the First World War (1914–8); a large number never returned home. With the absence of local men during this period it fell to a group of women to launch the Lynmouth lifeboat on 13 January 1915 when the *SS Mikasa* ran aground at Woody Bay – all nine crewmembers were saved.

The Second World War

At the start of the Second World War (1939–45) North Devon was a vulnerable target for invasion by enemy forces, resulting in territorial units from the British Army being sent to defend the coastline. German U-boats were often spotted surfacing in the Bristol Channel; at dusk locals would witness them sending dinghies ashore to secluded coves on the Exmoor coast to fetch spring water. At Girt Down Farm near Combe Martin a bomb dropped by a German aircraft damaged buildings and killed a cow – thankfully the only home front fatality in Combe Martin – while on 24 July 1940 a German dive-bomber was shot down over Martinhoe Common by three Spitfire pilots scrambled from South Wales. Despite these rare attacks by enemy aircraft, North Devon was considered a safe haven for the hundreds of evacuees who were sent to the region from large cities.

Assault Training Centre

By 1943 Allied forces were gearing up to attack occupied northern France, which would culminate in the D-Day invasion of 6 June 1944. American forces were assigned the stretch of coastline between Crow Point and Morte Point to train the US Army for Operation Overlord (D-Day) due to its similarities to the Normandy coast. Within a short period of time the area was transformed into the US Assault Training Center (ATC), with Woolacombe Bay Hotel its administrative headquarters. By the time the first American troops arrived in September 1943 the

Below Training on the Demolition Range at the Assault Training Center. This was located in 'Area C', which spanned the central part of Braunton Burrows. All live firing was seaward

Right A Motor Pool at the Assault Training Center. Part of 'Area D', on the northern part of Braunton Burrows

coastal area was strewn with Nissen huts and tents to accommodate the influx of military personnel, temporary roads and observation houses had been constructed, and numerous training aids, such as dummy pillboxes and replica concrete landing crafts, had been built within the landscape – the remains of many of these can still be seen today.

The 10-mile stretch of coastline that made up the ATC was divided into zones, each utilised for different training exercises: Morte Point was used for seaborne artillery practice, resulting in the slates becoming pockmarked with shell craters, which are still evident today (along with the occasional discovery of shrapnel fragments); the sheer sea cliffs at Baggy Point were used for cliff-scaling exercises; dummy landing crafts at Braunton Burrows and Woolacombe Warren were used to train the men on how to embark and disembark before they progressed to using real amphibious vehicles in the surf at Croyde Bay; and Woolacombe Sands, with its topography, tides and sand consistency similar to Omaha beach in Normandy, was used for dramatic full-scale attack exercises.

The ATC was an extensive, short-lived but highly effective military facility that trained a total of 22,500 American troops in amphibious assault tactics over a six-month period. Today a memorial on Woolacombe's esplanade commemorates all the Americans that trained at the ATC for the Normandy landings – a military strategy that marked the beginning of the end of the war in Europe.

Agriculture

For thousands of years North Devon's land has been farmed, with agriculture integral to the local economy and rural community, as well as helping to shape the beautiful landscape we see today.

Early farming

Evidence of prehistoric hut circles and field systems, such as those on Holdstone Down in West Exmoor, which date from the Late Neolithic to Late Bronze Age (c.2350BC to 700BC), reveals that early farmers settled on the land in small enclosures to grow crops and keep livestock.

However, the most significant indication of historical farming in North Devon dates to the Middle Ages (c.AD410 to 1540), with aerial surveys revealing a number of earthwork remains of medieval open-field systems. These field systems are indicative of the arable farming methods of the time, whereby unenclosed land was separated into long narrow strips, with no obvious field boundaries, and allocated to individual farmers or peasant families. To accommodate North Devon's steep slopes many of these strip fields were terraced to form narrow ledges known as 'strip lynchets'. Examples of such field systems can be seen in the cliff-top fields above Gawlish Cliffs, near East Titchberry, and on the slopes of Little Hangman in West Exmoor. An extensive area of medieval, and possibly post-medieval, field systems also survives on the open moorland around Countisbury Common, near Kipscombe Farm, and on the headland at Baggy Point.

Modern farming

Over time North Devon's landscape has influenced the direction that farming has taken. In the late 19th century there was a boom in market gardening, with the sheltered fields on the steep south-facing slopes around Combe Martin providing the perfect conditions for growing strawberries and other soft fruits. Today, livestock farming accounts for the majority of farming in North Devon. Both dairy and beef cattle – notably North Devon Reds, a gentle but hardy local breed – graze the region's uplands, lowlands and coastal grasslands, while sheep farming dominates in Exmoor's upland hills.

Throughout the UK modern agricultural practices, such as the use of fertilisers and pesticides, have damaged the landscape and threatened wildlife species. To protect the future biodiversity of the natural environment it's becoming increasingly important for local landowners, such as the National Trust, to work closely with farmers to develop and encourage sustainable and nature-friendly farming methods. For the Trust this is about managing in-hand farms such as Kipscombe and working in partnership with tenant farmers on a common cause: placing nature at the heart of farming. This is being achieved through both innovative and traditional land management methods, such as grazing specialist livestock on Trust-owned land. Throughout North Devon, the Trust is introducing extensive grazing with a variety of livestock and in a number of habitats. The many grazing animals will eat different plants, and larger animals like cattle and ponies will trample down overgrown areas. This diverse grazing creates space for a variety of plant species, which in turn will support a greater array of wildlife. Within North Devon you might see: Hebridean sheep on Baggy Point, Highland Cattle on the Culm Grassland near Brownsham, Exmoor Ponies at Foreland Point on Exmoor and North Devon Red Cattle on the dunes at Woolacombe. All are helping us to manage for the good of the wildlife.

The return of wildlife

A true test of the ability that nature-friendly farming can have to restore wildlife habitats would be the much-anticipated return of the chough to North Devon – a bird that has been absent for over 70 years following a loss of its habitat due to the lack of grazing on marginal cliff edges since the 1940s. Working in partnership with tenant farmers the Trust plans to reintroduce cattle grazing at key cliff-top sites, meaning this red-billed and red-legged member of the crow family may well become a familiar sight again on North Devon's cliffs.

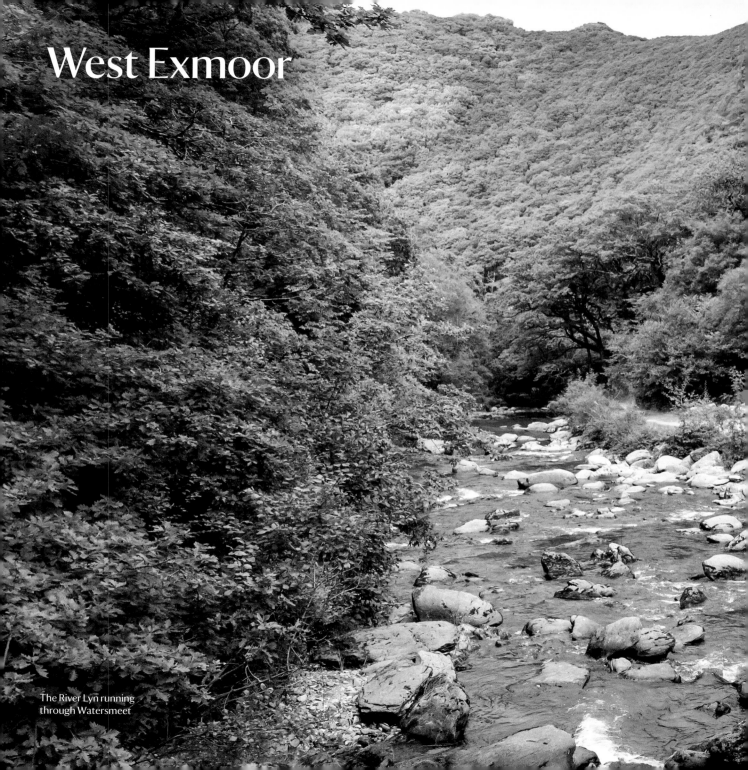

West Exmoor

The River Lyn running
through Watersmeet

The Hangmans and Wild Pear Beach

On the western fringe of Exmoor National Park lies an expanse of open coastal heathland stretching across some of the highest sea cliffs in the UK.

Mining heritage

This heathland habitat of the Hangman Hills attracts a rich abundance of flora and fauna, but hidden beneath the gorse, heather and bracken lie traces of the area's mining heritage (see pp. 8–9). Today the landscape is pitted with exploratory adits and mine shafts from an era when silver was the area's prominent mined metal. These mine workings had a great influence on the nearby village of Combe Martin, which saw its population soar during the mining heyday in the 19th century. But by the early 1900s Combe Martin's mining days were over, and the village instead became famous for the strawberries that flourished on the valley's sheltered, south-facing slopes.

The Hangman siblings

The towering cliffs of Little Hangman and Great Hangman make up the Hangman Hills that dominate the skyline above Combe Martin. Believed to have derived their name from the Celtic word *'an maen'*, roughly translated as 'stone hill', in late summer these twin summits are a magenta-and-yellow blanket of cross-leaved heath, ling and bell heather. Given to the National Trust in 1972, Great Hangman (1,043 feet/318m) is classed as England's highest sea cliff and is also the highest point on the South West Coast Path. From its cairn there are tremendous views of the surrounding landscape: across the Bristol Channel to South Wales, south-east to the Exmoor hills and west towards Lundy Island. Its sibling, Little Hangman (715 feet/218m), was acquired by the Trust in 1982. Running between Little and Great Hangman are the remains of a rifle range, visible today as a scrub-covered oval mound, used in the early 1900s to train volunteer infantrymen.

Wild Pear Beach

Below the towering cliffs of Little Hangman, and accessible down a very steep track signposted from the footpath, is the hidden gem of Wild Pear Beach. Wild Pear is a blissfully secluded and sheltered cove ideal for rockpooling at low tide. Due to its remoteness it has become a popular naturist haunt; for similar reasons it was a favoured location for smugglers who stored their contraband in the surrounding caves. The beach was closed to the public for many years following a landslip caused by fierce winter storms, but

repairs by the National Trust meant it was reopened in 2008. High above Wild Pear Beach was once a café that catered to walkers and served clotted cream and the famous Combe Martin strawberries from the 1920s up until the 1990s.

A medieval manor

Across the brow of the hill from Wild Pear Beach is the whitewashed building of West Challacombe, a beautifully restored 15th-century manor house now available to rent as holiday accommodation (see pp. 58–9). It was acquired by the National Trust in 1991, and during restoration of the building a magnificent oak hammer-beam roof was discovered in the upstairs sitting room – evidence indicates that the roof was built in the mid-15th century with timber felled between 1449 and 1474. Open days throughout the year allow the public to see this well-preserved medieval roof.

Above The interior of West Challacombe Manor, now a holiday cottage for most of the year

Centre Common heather, bell heather and western gorse on the Great Hangman

Left Hangman Hill café

Holdstone Down
and Trentishoe

Along the high cliffs between Combe Martin and Heddon's Mouth stretches one of the most remote sections of the South West Coast Path. If you're looking to escape to a wild, rugged and isolated landscape, this is the place to visit.

Coastal heathlands

Tracking east from Great Hangman, the land plunges down to Sherrycombe – a deep-cut valley where during the Second World War locals spotted sailors from German U-boats sourcing fresh water from the waterfall. The land then rises up and extends across the expanse of Holdstone Down and Trentishoe Down, which are designated Sites of Special Scientific Interest (SSSI) and Special Areas of Conservation (SAC) for their coastal heathlands that support a rich population of breeding birds, including Dartford warblers, peregrine falcons and stonechats.

These apparently unspoilt heathlands have been marked by human activity for millennia, with earthwork remains of Bronze Age hut circles, barrows and cairns. There are also remnants of mortar positions and shell casings lying beneath the heather and gorse from military exercises that took place on Holdstone Down during the 1940s.

Holdstone Down

The solitude and isolation experienced in this remote coastal landscape could have been ruined if ambitious plans to create a tourist resort on Holdstone Down had succeeded in the 1890s. At the time the moorland was divided into 143 plots, but only 50 plots were sold – today several bodies, including the National Trust, own the plots and the landscape remains wild and natural.

More recently Holdstone Down has become a pilgrimage site for UFO enthusiasts as a number of extra-terrestrial encounters are claimed to have taken place on its rounded summit, Holdstone Hill (1,145 feet/349m).

A valley of butterflies

In contrast to the exposed landscape of the Downs, the sheltered bracken-clad slopes and oak woodlands that make up Trentishoe Valley, bought by the National Trust in 1963, is a much gentler setting. It's at sites here, and elsewhere in the Heddon Valley, that the UK's rarest butterfly, the high brown fritillary, thrives in a managed habitat (see p. 62), with June and July being the best months to spot them. Commoner dark-green and silver-washed fritillaries abound, often feeding on wild Buddleia bushes in the valley bottom.

Opposite A view of Trentishoe Down, as seen from Holdstone Down

Below left The dark-green fritillary is the most commonly seen fritillary butterfly in the British Isles

Below centre A Dartford warbler upon yellow gorse, where they typically sit to sing

Below right A male stonechat perches on a gorse bush; a stonechat's call sounds like two stones being tapped together

Heddon Valley and Woody Bay

With its deep wooded river valley, towering rugged sea cliffs and sheltered slopes attracting rare butterflies, the varied landscape of Heddon Valley is a unique place to visit.

Located at the centre of the area of West Exmoor looked after by the National Trust, the site is designated a SSSI and SAC for its extensive sessile oak woodlands and coastal heaths.

Hunter's Inn

At the heart of Heddon Valley is Hunter's Inn, a picturesque hotel situated next to the River Heddon. Originally a thatched cottage, it morphed into a wayward watering hole serving ales to thirsty locals, but was tragically destroyed by fire in November 1895.

At the time the owner, a wealthy solicitor called Colonel Benjamin Lake, had constructed a three-mile scenic carriageway between Woody Bay and Hunter's Inn as part of his grand plan to establish a holiday resort at Woody Bay and, in 1897, Lake built an imposing new hotel on the site of the original thatched cottage. Designed to resemble a Swiss chalet, Hunter's Inn re-opened in 1906 and immediately attracted holidaymakers at a time when tourism was in its infancy. Today the hotel has mellowed into its tranquil surroundings and is still a popular rest stop for visitors. The National Trust acquired much of the land surrounding Hunter's Inn in 1990, and our shop and car- park are ideally positioned for visitors wishing to explore Heddon Valley.

Heddon's Mouth

Starting at Hunter's Inn is a mile-long riverside walk along the gorge-like Heddon's Mouth Cleave, where exposed scree slopes are indicative of a periglacial landscape created during the Pleistocene Ice Age (*c*.2.5 million to 11,700 years ago). The walk brings you to the rocky beach at Heddon's Mouth. This old smugglers' path was also the route once taken by mules laden with burnt limestone from the lime kiln located on the beach at Heddon's Mouth – the kiln was restored in 1982 by the National Trust, with further work carried out in 1991 to build a wall to protect it from storms and high tides.

Lime-loving plants, in particular spindle trees with their distinctive pink seedpods visible in winter, have established themselves along the path where fallen burnt limestone has 'sweetened' the acidic soil.

Woody Bay

Heddon Valley is the gateway to West Exmoor and there's no better introduction to this dynamic stretch of Exmoor's coastline than following the carriageway built by Lake in the 1890s along the windswept high cliffs to Woody Bay.

In summer the headlands at Highveer Point and Wringapeak are alive with breeding colonies of seabirds, including cormorants, fulmars, guillemots, kittiwakes and razorbills. A short detour off the carriageway brings you to the remains of a cliff-top Roman fortlet strategically positioned above Heddon's Mouth, which was briefly occupied in the 1st century AD (see p. 5). Just before reaching West Woodybay Wood, where ash, larch and birch grow among gnarled oak trees, a spectacular waterfall tumbles down the cliff at Hollow Brook Combe in a series of cascades before dropping over 650 feet (200 metres) into the sea.

The secluded cove of Woody Bay is a sanctuary. Its rocky beach, accessible via a steep zig-zag path, is surrounded by pristine woodlands of sessile oak and rare whitebeams. But things could have turned out very differently for this unspoilt corner of West Exmoor if Lake's extravagant plans to turn the area into a tourist resort had been successful. Little remains of Lake's failed enterprise, but look hard enough and you'll spot relics: under the cliffs are the remains of a changing room and swimming pool built into the rocks, and a concrete jetty is evidence of Lake's short-lived and farcical pier, which was too short to allow steamers to dock at low tide. After getting severely damaged in storms, it was demolished in 1902, a year after Lake was sentenced to 12 years in prison for fraud.

In 1965 the National Trust bought 49 hectares (120 acres) of Woody Bay through its Neptune Coastline Campaign (previously the Enterprise Neptune Appeal), and under its ownership the woodland has been managed to encourage a healthy diversity of plant and animal life.

Above Looking down on the beach at Woody Bay

Left Heddon's Mouth

Watersmeet Estate

In the late 18th century, the scenery surrounding Lynmouth attracted key figures in the Romantic Movement: Byron, Coleridge, Shelley, Southey and Wordsworth. Southey coined the phrase 'Little Switzerland' after likening the landscape to the Alps. In 1812 Shelley honeymooned at Lynmouth with his teenage bride Harriet, and drafted 'Queen Mab' and his infamous 'Declaration of Rights' there.

The dramatic coastline, wooded gorges and tumbling rivers proved irresistible to writers seeking creative inspiration from the natural world and continues to attract visitors today.

East Lyn Valley

Central to this inspirational landscape is the East Lyn Valley, where steep slopes of ancient oak woodland line the meandering East Lyn River and its tributary, Hoar Oak Water, as they tumble and cascade over boulders and under bridges to reach the sea at Lynmouth. Lyn is believed to derive from the Old English word *'hlynn'*, meaning 'torrent'. The fast-flowing East Lyn River is regarded as the best river in the country for Atlantic salmon, with adult salmon often seen leaping upstream to spawn during the winter months. With over 40 miles (64km) of footpaths offering interesting and diverse walking routes, it's a walker's paradise; the plentiful plants and wildlife make it a haven for nature lovers; while the wild, natural environment is perfect for those seeking relief from their urban lives.

The East Lyn Valley's extensive woodland is the largest remaining Ancient Semi-Natural Woodland (ASNW) in the south west and a designated SSSI. Although dominated by sessile oak, the wooded valley is also home to a number of rare whitebeams only found growing in Exmoor, including the interestingly named 'No Parking' whitebeam. First discovered in a lay-by near Watersmeet in the 1930s with such a sign affixed to it, it was formally identified as a new tree species in 2009 and there are reported to be at least 110 trees in the Watersmeet area (98 per cent of the world's population).

For centuries these woodlands were felled and coppiced, with the timber used to fuel lime kilns, and to make charcoal and tan bark, as well as pit props for use in Welsh coal mines.

Above A footbridge over the river at Watersmeet

Wildlife at East Lyn

The National Trust acquired much of the land surrounding the East Lyn River between the 1930s and 1990s. Under its ownership careful management of the woods has created rich habitats that host many wildflower species, such as the rare Irish spurge and locally rare stone bramble, and communities of localised 'old woodland' lichen species. There is also a diverse population of breeding woodland birds, including pied flycatchers, redstarts and wood warblers. In the late 19th century an abundance of ferns, which are still evident today, made the East Lyn Valley a world-famous hunting ground for Victorian fern collectors (there was a huge craze for ferns and fern-hunting during the period).

Above left A sign marking Crook Pool, a pool just above Watersmeet named for its resemblance to a shepherd's crook

Above right Redstarts spend little time at ground level

The Lynmouth Flood

On 15 August 1952 a devastating flood hit Lynmouth. Thirty-four people tragically lost their lives and more than 100 buildings were destroyed. A gentle riverside walk along the East Lyn River shows some of the flood's devastation. A mile (1.6km) upstream from Lynmouth, the foundations are all that remain of Lynrock Mineral Water Company, a bottling factory that opened in 1911 and had its heyday during the 1920s and 1930s. It was owned by the Attree brothers, who lived at Myrtleberry, a short distance up the river, and produced naturally sparkling mineral water (reputedly with 'radio-active' properties that could cure gout) from a natural spring that still runs from a small hollow in the rock face. Another flood casualty was a hydro-electric power station that used the East Lyn's fast-flowing water to generate electricity for Lynmouth's residents during much of the early 20th century. After being damaged in the floods, the station was later demolished to widen the river.

Watersmeet: Countisbury and the Foreland

The large expanse of open heathland that stretches out from the elevated hamlet of Countisbury is a great place to see Exmoor ponies grazing among a colourful mosaic of heather and gorse.

On a clear night, it is also an ideal location to marvel at the night sky: Exmoor National Park was designated Europe's first International Dark Sky Reserve in autumn 2011.

Whichever route you take to reach Countisbury, it's a challenging climb. You can follow the coastal footpath as it snakes steeply from Lynmouth and then gradually ascends along the open coastline – the stunning views along Exmoor's coastline a welcome distraction. Alternatively you can go by vehicle, up the daunting one-in-five gradient of Countisbury Hill.

Thankfully an old coaching inn, the Blue Ball, is well positioned at the top of the climb to cater for tired and thirsty passersby, as it has been for over three centuries. And if that's not enough, the wide-ranging views at the top, especially from the stone hut at Butter Hill (990 feet/302m) – west across Lynmouth Bay to Great Hangman, east to Hurlstone Point beyond Porlock Bay and north across the Bristol Channel to South Wales – certainly make the hike worthwhile.

The National Trust at Countisbury

The National Trust obtained a large proportion of the land surrounding Countisbury in 1971, including The Foreland, an exposed triangular headland that extends out to Foreland Point, the most northerly point in Devon, where Foreland lighthouse clings to the cliff edge. Since its acquisition by the National Trust in 1993 the grassland and farmland east of Countisbury, around Kipscombe Hill, has been allowed to regenerate. Plants such as tormentil, heath milkwort and heath bedstraw now grow among pockets of gorse and heather, and birds such as linnets, wheatears and whinchats make their nests here during the summer breeding season. Despite a recent national decline in numbers, skylarks are abundant in Exmoor with pairs known to nest in the farmland surrounding Kipscombe Farm – from early spring and throughout the summer their beautiful song can be heard filling the air.

Right Exmoor ponies graze on Kipscombe Hill

Far right The view to Wind Hill, Countisbury

Watersmeet House

The jewel of Watersmeet Estate is Watersmeet House, an idyllic fishing lodge nestled among the woodlands at the confluence of the East Lyn River and Hoar Oak Water.

Built in 1832 by Reverend Walter Stevenson Halliday, using stone from the nearby quarry, the design of the building was heavily influenced by a popular architecture manual of the time, *Rural Architecture: Being a Series of Designs for Ornamental Cottages* (1822). The lodge closely resembles Glenthorne House, Halliday's 1829 gothic-style manor house near Countisbury.

A self-confessed romantic and a devotee of the Romantic poets who visited the area, Halliday had a Wordsworth poem (written about the Lake District) inscribed above the entrance door of the fishing lodge – it can still be seen today underneath a statue of a boar's head, which features on the Halliday family crest.

> The spot was made by nature for herself:
> The travellers know it not, and 'twill remain
> Unknown to them: but it is beautiful:
> And if a man should plant his cottage near,
> Should sleep beneath the shelter of its trees,
> And blend its waters with his daily meal,
> He would so love it, that in his death-hour
> Its image would survive among his thoughts.

Above The Wordsworth poem inscribed above the door at Watersmeet House

Unsettled beginnings

Many locals considered the elaborate building an eyesore when it was built, and only four years after it was completed Halliday sold the lodge to wealthy landowner John James Scott for £1,200. A few years later it was back in Halliday's possession when Scott sold all his assets in the area. Another failed attempt to sell Watersmeet in 1841 left Halliday no option but to rent the now virtually abandoned property as a labourers' cottage from the 1850s. Mine adits near the lodge are evidence of Halliday's failed attempt to mine iron ore in 1870, two years before his death, and a pair of lime kilns a few hundred metres from the lodge would have served the wider Watersmeet Estate during the 19th century.

The National Trust's acquisition

In 1932 the National Trust began the process of acquiring Watersmeet House from the Halliday family, with the Lynton and Lynmouth Preservation of Local Natural Beauty Association playing an instrumental role in raising funds to purchase the lodge and surrounding land for £8,500. The sale was completed in 1934 and following renovations Watersmeet House was formally opened as a National Trust property in 1936.

Watersmeet House was closed for six months in September 2016 to allow for extensive work to be done to replace the entire roof – the project required 4,300 new slate tiles and cost £150,000, generously funded by Trust donations and a grant.

Tea wars

Today the former fishing lodge Watersmeet House is a popular tea-garden well known for its cream teas. Records show its days as a tea-room began as early as the 1870s when tenants John Nercombe and his family sold refreshments to passersby. At the time they weren't the only, or indeed the most popular, tea-room in the area; that accolade went to William Attree – father of the Attree brothers, owners of the Lynrock Mineral Water Company (see p. 25) – who was running a thriving business across the river at Myrtleberry selling refreshments to adventurous Edwardians exploring the East Lyn Valley. The shrewd businessman even set up kiosks – complete with dancing monkeys and glamorous tea ladies, and selling the popular ginger beer from the Attree brothers' nearby bottling factory – directly opposite his competitor, and on the more accessible side of the river than Watersmeet House.

Things came to a head between the two tea-rooms in 1911 when Nercombe took Attree to court accusing him of deliberately damaging the only bridge across the river allowing access to Watersmeet House. As comeuppance for Attree's dodgy deeds, the fortunes of his tea-room declined with the arrival of the motorcar to Exmoor in the 1920s. Despite many attempts by Attree to gain permission to build a car-park at his Myrtleberry tea-room, it was declined due to space restraints. This time the fortune fell to Nercombe when a car-park was built near to Watersmeet House, encouraging a steady flow of customers down the steps (now a slope) and across the wooden bridge to his tea-room – a journey many visitors still make today.

Centre The river flowing past Watersmeet House in autumn

Things to see and do in West Exmoor

Above **Discover the Heddon's Mouth path**

Canoe along the East Lyn

Between 1 October and 31 March, when water levels are high enough, expert canoeists can follow the East Lyn River downstream from Watersmeet House on its journey to the sea at Lynmouth. There are two access points, one at Watersmeet House and one at Lyn Rock, with one set exit point at Woodside Bridge.

Follow a butterfly trail

Between June and July follow a butterfly walk in Heddon Valley (either self-guided or join an organised walk with a National Trust ranger). If you don't manage to see the rare high brown fritillary, you should see the dark-green or silver-washed fritillaries and you're guaranteed superb scenery in one of the most beautiful woodland coastal combes in Exmoor.

Walk from Heddon's Mouth to Woody Bay

This six-mile (9.6km) circular walk follows an historic 19th-century carriageway along high cliffs with breathtaking views along the dramatic West Exmoor coast and across the Bristol Channel to South Wales. Along the way you will pass a cliff-top Roman fortlet, see a spectacular waterfall cascading down the cliff to the sea, and walk through ancient oak woodlands.

Enjoy a cream tea

Having supplied refreshments to passersby for over 100 years, Watersmeet House knows how to cater for tired walkers and thirsty visitors. Perched next to the fast-flowing East Lyn River and surrounded by oak trees, the peaceful garden is a stunning setting to enjoy a well-earned cream tea.

Go stargazing

On a clear night head to Holdstone Hill to witness a simply stunning night sky. Exmoor's magical dark skies are protected as an International Dark Sky Reserve and many astronomical sights can be seen through the naked eye, and even more can be discovered through a telescope or binoculars. You will not be disappointed.

Spend a night outdoors

There are plenty of options to experience a night outdoors in West Exmoor. From mid-July until mid-August you can pitch a tent in a meadow in Heddon Valley on a first-come, first-served basis, while all-year-round two National Trust bothies – one at Foreland Point and the other at Heddon Orchard – are ideal for those wanting to escape the modern world for a night or two for some back-to-basics living.

Go fungi foraging

By autumn the woodlands in Heddon Valley are rife with fungi of all shapes, sizes and colours. We advise against picking fungi yourself, but to learn more about them and to find out which are edible and which are best avoided, you can join an expert on a fungi walk organised by the National Trust.

Above Stop for a cream tea at Watersmeet House

Left See if you can spot the rare high brown fritillary on a butterfly trail

Croyde, Woolacombe and Ilfracombe

Sunset over Baggy Point

Croyde Bay and Baggy Point

The rocky coastline surrounding the high promontory of Baggy Point is a geological marvel, while its landscape hides traces of prehistoric human activity and a variety of habitats rich in botanical species. It's also an adventurer's paradise for those seeking coastal and water-based activities.

Croyde

Sandwiched between the headlands of Downend and Baggy Point, the west-facing beach of Croyde draws in rolling Atlantic waves making it one of the best surf spots in the UK. At low tide an expanse of rocky shore on either side of the sandy beach is superb for rockpooling, with a number of seashore species, such as blennies, dog-whelks, limpets, sea anemones and winkles, discoverable in tidal pools. The remains of two 19th-century lime kilns – one used as a public shelter on the beach front – reveal traces of Croyde's industrial past; a ramp leading on to the beach, along with grooves embedded in the foreshore rocks, tracks the route taken by carts loaded with limestone. Elsewhere, remnants of concrete structures point to the part Croyde played during the training of American troops prior to D-Day during the Second World War (see p. 12).

A National Trust car-park at the north end of Croyde beach – next to Sandleigh Tea Room, managed by National Trust tenants – is perfectly placed for visiting the beach or exploring Baggy Point.

Baggy Point

Walk to the furthest point of Baggy Point and, on a clear day, you will be rewarded with a stunning coastal vista: to the west the long arm of Hartland Peninsula, with the outline of Hartland lighthouse perched at the far end and the tall cliff-top radar dome clearly visible; straight ahead on the horizon the low profile of Lundy Island; and to the east Morte Point and, if you're lucky, Gower Peninsula in South Wales. The panoramic views are equally spectacular from the summit of Middleborough Hill, the highest point on the headland. Previously overhead cables blighted the view, but in 2009 the National Trust succeeded with an ambitious project to bury the cables, enhancing the area's natural beauty for both visitors and locals.

Rising abruptly 197 feet (60 metres) above sea level, the craggy-faced promontory of Baggy Point – formed of fine-grained sandstone rock, known as Baggy Sandstones or Baggy Beds, laid down during the Upper Devonian Period (c.385 to 359 million years ago) – attracts walkers, trail runners and those seeking the perfect sunset-viewing spot. Climbers are often seen scaling the sheer cliffs, while further below coasteerers explore the rocky coastline (not activities for the inexperienced). During nesting season (March to June) the west-facing cliffs are alive with seabirds – cormorants, fulmars, guillemots, gulls, herrings, shags and razorbills are known to nest here – while grey seals are regular visitors to the waters around Baggy Point.

Baggy Leap

Below the headland lie the treacherous waters of Baggy Leap, a sunken reef and the final resting place of *HMS Weazle*, wrecked in 1799 (see p. 6). A tall, white coastguard pole, restored by the National Trust in 2016, stands on the headland as a reminder of the dangers of the sea. Built to represent a ship's mast, it was used in the 1930s to train coastguards in the use of rocket life-saving apparatus and to practise rescues with a breeches buoy, a land-based rescue technique used when seas were too rough to launch a lifeboat.

Far left The beach at Baggy Point

Left The Milky Way above Croyde beach

Below Coasteering at Baggy Point (we recommend only undertaking this activity as part of a led group)

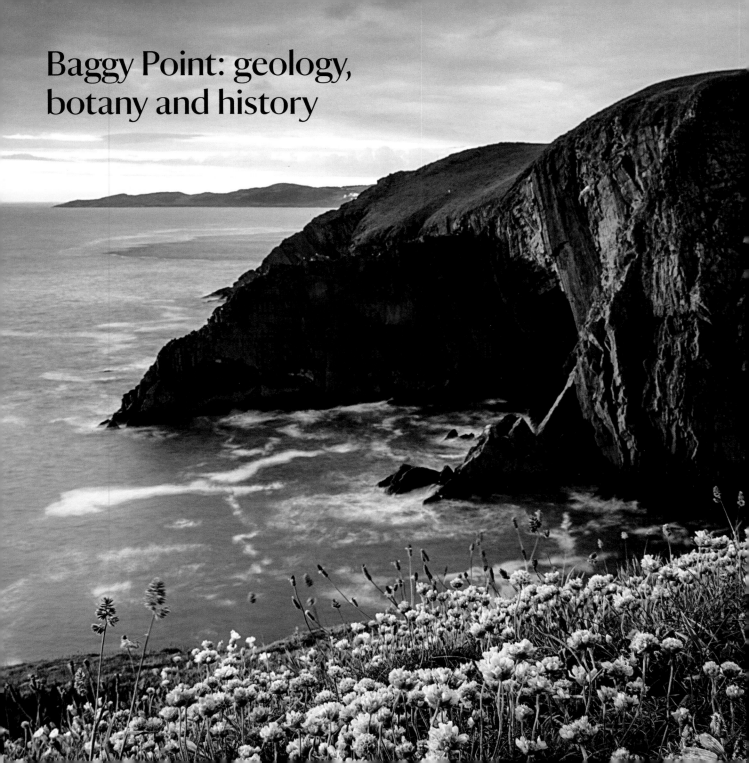

Baggy Point: geology, botany and history

Baggy Point is a designated Site of Special Scientific Interest (SSSI) for both its geodiversity and its botanical features.

Its unique coastal geology features wave-cut rocky platforms, raised beaches and large glacial erratic boulders (non-native rocks) – all formed thousands of years ago by changing sea levels and fluctuations in the climate.

In late spring and into summer, maritime wildflowers thrive in the variety of habitats: the cliff slopes are a colourful bank of thrift, sea campion, wild carrot, hairy bird's foot trefoil and kidney vetch; in crevices and on ledges you'll find sea beet, rock samphire and rock sea spurry; while sea kale and sea stock grow along the shore. A National Trust tenant farmer grazes a flock of hardy black-fleeced Hebridean sheep on the steep slopes to keep the maritime heath free from scrub to encourage a more species-rich coastal habitat.

The history
The discovery of prehistoric artefacts points to there being human activity on Baggy Point for thousands of years (see p. 4). Signs of ancient farming are embedded in the broad plateau that tops the promontory and evidence of medieval open field systems and enclosed pastures date back to the late 18th century. Hoe Wall, the dry-stone wall running down the spine of the headland, was once the boundary of the medieval strip fields; today it's covered in many lichen species, most noticeably the green-grey tufts of sea ivory lichen.

The Private
Near to Hoe Wall lie the remains of dummy pillboxes used by American troops during their D-Day training (see p. 12). Look closely and you will see a name, A. A. Augustine, inscribed on the wall of one of the pillboxes. In the autumn of 1943, while tasked with building one of the ten pillboxes on Baggy Point, 24-year-old Alfred Augustine, a private in the 146th Engineer Combat Battalion, scratched his name into the wet cement. He was killed on Omaha beach on 6 June 1944, one of 10,000 Allied troops killed or wounded during the D-Day invasion.

Baggy House
The Hyde sisters, Florence and Constantine, whose family lived at Baggy House, gifted much of Baggy Point to the National Trust in 1939. Today a privately owned modernist house has replaced the original house. On the side of the coast path a lichen-covered whale bone is displayed as a legacy to the Hydes; it was preserved by the family after the whale was washed ashore at Croyde beach in 1915. Near Baggy House is a natural harbour and slipway, carved into the rocks by the Hyde family.

Opposite Baggy Cove

Henry Williamson
During the 1920s a frequent visitor to Baggy Point was the author and naturalist Henry Williamson, who lived in nearby Georgeham. The headland was a favoured haunt and is one of many North Devon landmarks that feature in his classic tale, *Tarka the Otter* (1927). Written from an otter's viewpoint, the book takes readers on a journey through

a landscape little changed since Williamson first penned his words over a century ago. In chapter eight, his meticulous research and observations of the natural world see the main protagonist, Tarka, fishing for bass at Bag Leap near the 'shellcrusted cannon and gear' of *HMS Weazle*, and Greymuzzle, the bitch-otter, exploring the 'limp-studded rocks of Bag Hole' and climbing up 'springy clumps of sea-thrift'.

Morte Bay

It is thanks to the generosity of Miss Rosalie Chichester, the last heir to nearby Arlington Court (also National Trust), that most of the land at Woolacombe and Mortehoe is managed and protected by the National Trust.

In 1909 Miss Chichester gifted the headland at Morte Point to the Trust – the first North Devon coastal property the charity acquired – in memory of her parents, Sir Bruce and Lady Chichester. Potter's Hill was given to the Trust in 1935 to commemorate the Silver Jubilee of George V, while the remaining swathes of Chichester-owned land at Woolacombe, along with the village of Mortehoe, were left to the Trust in Rosalie's will and were acquired after her death in 1949.

Woolacombe

Approaching Woolacombe Sands on foot from Baggy Point, you're greeted with a breathtaking vista: a curved expanse of white-sand beach, almost two miles (3.2km) long, running the breadth of Morte Bay – the sheltered beach of Putsborough at the southern end and the popular seaside resort of Woolacombe at the busier northern end – with the tapering headland of Morte Point slicing between the expansive sky and vast seascape.

This is the gateway to an adventurer's playground, where you're spoilt for choice for land and water-based coastal activities, from surfing or stand-up paddleboarding in the Atlantic waves, to walking or running the length of the beach or along the undulating coastal footpath. For less active adventures you can enjoy building sandcastles, exploring rock pools or bathing in the sea; or maybe you'd prefer to just sit in the dunes appreciating the peace and tranquility with a good book.

Woolacombe Warren

Behind the long sandy beach is a system of sand dunes known as Woolacombe Warren, which, over the years, have suffered both natural and manmade erosion; if you look carefully you can see evidence of a golf course, in use until 1939, while overgrown concrete blocks are all that remain of dummy landing crafts used by the American troops during their D-Day training (see p. 12). Today the National Trust carefully manages the dunes by controlled grazing of the scrub (see p. 63), helped by the many rabbits living in the appropriately named Warren – as

a result the habitat is thriving with dune-loving wildflowers, such as pyramidal orchids and bee orchids, and rare Portland spurge and sea holly. Behind Woolacombe Warren, and running parallel to the beach, is Marine Drive, a legacy of the Chichester family who built the roadway in 1906, planning to reach all the way to Putsborough. It was never completed and today is used as a car-park – and is another great sunset-viewing spot.

Woolacombe Down

The dunes are backed by Woolacombe Down, a former sea cliff now covered in coconut-scented gorse scrub and patches of heather, which paint the steep slopes yellow and purple during the summer months. Along with its role as an elevated launch pad for paragliders, the Down is teeming with an array of wildlife hiding beneath the scrub, including adders, green hairstreak butterflies, lizards, leaf beetles and rare micro-moths.

At the northern end of the Down rises a small, conical hill known as Potter's Hill. It's a short, steep hike to the top, following an overgrown zig-zag path cut into the hill in 1911 to commemorate the coronation of George V, but the climb is certainly worth it for the extensive, uninterrupted views across Morte Bay, flanked by the distinctive headlands of Morte Point and Baggy Point, and out towards the long profile of Lundy Island on the horizon.

Above Cows grazing at Woolacombe Warren

Left Rosalie, Lady Chichester of Arlington Court, who left significant portions of land in this area to the National Trust

The ghostly Woolacombe wanderer

According to folklore the ghost of nobleman and knight, Sir William de Tracey, roams Woolacombe Sands on stormy nights – local legend has it he's serving penance for murdering Thomas à Becket in December 1170 by weaving an impossible chain of sand along the length of the beach.

Morte Point

A steep climb from Woolacombe's esplanade brings you to Mortehoe, a pretty village that can trace its origins back to the 1086 Domesday Book, when it was recorded as a settlement of three farms.

It remained a small rural farming community up until the late 1800s, when the opening of the now defunct Ilfracombe branch railway in 1874 brought hordes of Victorian tourists to Woolacombe and Mortehoe. The village's rich heritage is documented in Mortehoe Museum, which is housed in a listed National Trust building in the centre of the village.

Shipwrecks and 'Mortemen'
Much of Mortehoe's history centres around the numerous shipwrecks caught out by the treacherous waters and rocky coastline around Morte Point, and the ensuing brutal conduct of wrecking by 'Mortemen', greatly feared by sailors (see p. 7). In the winter of 1852 five ships were wrecked near the Point – it's no surprise that for centuries people believed the headland was named after the French word 'mort', meaning 'death', although it's more likely to have derived from a Saxon word meaning 'short' or 'stumpy', referring to the shape of the headland.

Heritage and habitats
Despite its past reputation as a graveyard for ships, Morte Point is a gem to visit and only a short walk from Mortehoe. Not only does it feel remote and other-worldly, especially when you stand on the dramatic jagged-edged slates at its far end – some scarred by bullets fired during D-Day training – but it's also a designated SSSI for its maritime heath and coastal habitats, which attract an array of maritime flowers and breeding seabirds, while the inland grassland is home to birds such as stonechats and meadow pipits. A coastguard lookout hut was built on the highest elevation of Morte Point in 1914, at the start of the Great War, to keep watch over the Bristol Channel for German U-boats and, after the war, to ease the number of vessels caught out in the dangerous waters. It was in use until the 1960s and demolished in 1982; a plaque inscribed with the names of those who 'waited and watched, guarding our coast' sits on its original site.

Above Meadow pipits have a familiar, high, piping call

Right Morte Bay

Rockham Beach

Along the stretch of coastline between Morte Point and Bull Point you'll find a hidden treasure: Rockham Beach. This secluded cove is the perfect escape from the crowds at Woolacombe. Its remote location, fully exposed to the wild Atlantic sea, has meant it has borne the brunt of many winter storms – a landslip after the brutal storms of winter 2013–14 closed the beach for two years, but with help from the National Trust the steep steps were rebuilt and access was restored. A reminder of Rockham Bay's savage nature is clearly visible on the beach when remnants from the steamship *SS Collier*, shipwrecked nearby in 1914, can be seen at low tide (see p. 6). The ever-observant writer Henry Williamson used the beach as the place where the protagonist in his novel, *Tarka the Otter*, picks up the scent of his mate, White-tip, 'where the rusted plates of wrecked ships lay in pools'.

The Morte Slates and Beds

Once you leave Morte Point and follow the coast path towards Bull Point you enter a wild and rugged landscape, made all the more dramatic by the distinctive sharp-angled rock formations. Known as Morte Slates, these pale grey glossy slates, slashed with white quartz veins, are part of the Morte Beds – sedimentary rocks laid down during the Devonian Period (*c.*417–354 million years ago) and tipped near vertical by movements in the Earth's crust 300 million years ago – that run from Woolacombe to Lee Bay. Keep an eye out for grey seals, which are frequently seen bobbing in the water or basking in the sunny sheltered inlets – a well-positioned bench overlooking Whiting Cove is a perfect viewing spot.

Bull Point, Lee Bay and Ilfracombe

Brandy Cove Point, Breakneck Point, Damage Cliffs – along the north-facing stretch of coastline between Bull Point and Ilfracombe the names of coastal features are evocative of the smuggling and wrecking that was rife along this coast during the late 18th and early 19th centuries.

Bull Point

Following the undulating coast path towards the small headland of Bull Point, either eastward from Morte Point or westward from Lee Bay, the white tower of Bull Point lighthouse intermittently pops into view. The lighthouse was originally built in 1879 in response to a petition to counter the loss of life from shipwrecks and from the barbaric actions of lawless wreckers. In September 1972, after 100 years in operation, disaster struck: a large chunk of the cliff crashed into the sea taking the lighthouse engine room with it. A temporary light tower serviced the area until a new automated lighthouse was built three years later. The rocky headland of Bull Point itself is a good place for a mid-walk break to rest your legs before tackling the undulating coastal footpath.

The smugglers of Lee Bay

The small village of Lee, nestled in a remote and rugged combe, is known for its fuchsias that set the hedgerows ablaze with scarlet flowers during the flowering season, as well as an infamous smuggler, Hannibal Richards. Originally a member of the notorious Cruel Coppinger's smuggling gang from Morwenstow in North Cornwall, Richards moved to Lee in 1789 and headed a gang of smugglers that operated out of the village. Nearby Sandy Cove was an ideal spot for the smuggling gang to secretly land contraband; legend has it that one of the caves above this cove was Richards' look-out point and where the lucky smuggler hid when the rest of his gang were captured during a raid. It's said he lived in the Old Mill House, now a private residence. As you walk down the old smugglers' track to reach this hidden cove it is easy to conjure up visions of midnight landings and imagine the smell of brandy in the air.

Above A watercolour painting of Torrs Walk by Algernon Peckover dated 4 June 1884. Algernon was a member of the family who lived at Peckover House, Cambridgeshire, now a National Trust property

Left A view of Bull Point

Far left Bull Point Lighthouse at night

Bennett's Mouth and Kinever Valley

From Bull Point a short walk brings you to the enclosed cove of Bennett's Mouth, a peaceful getaway from the busier beaches at Woolacombe. The best time to visit is at low tide when its rocky foreshore is full of rock pools brimming with marine life, while the higher freshwater pools are home to toad spawn in spring and covered in agile pondskaters in summer.

In contrast to the exposed coastal environment at Bennett's Mouth, the steep-sided Kinever Valley rises behind the cove and is a sheltered woodland haven home to a variety of breeding and wintering birds. Further along the coast, just before Lee Bay, lies Hilly Mouth, one of the best – and perhaps more hidden – spots in North Devon to see an abundance of wildflowers. In early spring the area is a mesmerising sea of yellow primroses, while later in spring and into summer it's an excellent location for bluebells and orchids.

Torrs Walk

Tourism has been a mainstay of Ilfracombe since visitors first flocked to the seaside resort by paddle steamers in Victorian times. In 1888 Torrs Walk, a steep zig-zag walk, was carved into the cliff face on the western edge of the town – for a toll of one penny, Victorian visitors could follow the scenic walk up to a refreshment pavilion and viewing spot on an elevated plateau. Today it will cost you nothing apart from some leg power to follow Torrs Walk to the toposcope at the summit – and to a fine view along the coast to Lee Bay and back over to the harbour town of Ilfracombe – but you will have to bring your own refreshments as the pavilion was demolished in 1964. The National Trust acquired the undulating pastureland, rich in both wildflowers and bird life, at the top of Torrs Walk, known as The Torrs, in 1967. Along with its amazing views, it's a peaceful spot within easy reach of Ilfracombe's bustling tourist hub.

Things to see and do at Croyde, Woolacombe and Ilfracombe

Go surfing

The Atlantic waves crashing onto the beaches at Croyde, Woolacombe and Putsborough attract surfers all year round. With strong rip currents Croyde is more suitable for experienced surfers, whereas Woolacombe is perfect for beginners and the sheltered break at Putsborough is popular with longboarders.

Go rockpooling

The rocky foreshores on many of the beaches along this stretch of coastline are great for discovering seashore species hiding in rock pools at low tide. Throughout July and August, join a National Trust ranger on an organised Rockpool Ramble at Combesgate beach to become adept at identifying a starfish from a seahare.

Watch the sunset

Standing at the furthest point of Baggy Point watching the sun setting over the Atlantic Ocean with the silhouette of Lundy Island on the horizon is a truly magical experience. An optional extra ingredient is a pod of dolphins leaping out of the water; you never know, you could get lucky!

Walk Morte Point to Bull Point

Get away from the crowds on this challenging six mile (9.6km) circular walk that takes in dramatic scenery of cliffs, rocky headlands and sandy bays. Bring a pair of binoculars as the coastline between Morte Point and Bull Point lighthouse is a popular haunt for grey seals and hovering kestrels.

Enjoy a cream tea

Pause for a delicious homemade cream tea in the beautiful walled garden at Sandleigh Tea Room next to Croyde beach, run by National Trust tenants. The Town Farmhouse B&B in the heart of Mortehoe village also serves cream teas in its garden between Easter and September.

Opt for pedal power

Follow a gentle 2.8-mile (4.5km) bike route along a quiet road from Mortehoe before following a private lane to the rocky headland at Bull Point, where you can enjoy a picnic near the lighthouse with an uninterrupted view across the Atlantic before returning to Mortehoe – a great activity for beginner cyclists.

Run to Lee Bay

Challenge yourself with a hilly 6.3-mile (10km) run along the South West Coast Path from Ilfracombe to Lee following the National Trust's Trust10 trail route. The out-and-back route starts with a climb up the zig-zag path at Torrs Walk before continuing along an undulating coastal route with spectacular views to reach the secluded cove at Lee Bay. (For more information: nationaltrust.org.uk/woolacombe/trails/ trust10-ilfracombe-to-lee)

Go paragliding

If you're feeling adventurous, and have a head for heights and prefer a bird's-eye-view of the coastline you can take off from the summit of Woolacombe Down and soar over Morte Bay. Novices can undertake tandem flights with Fly Like A Bird (flylikeabird.co.uk), but solo flights should only be attempted by experienced paragliders.

Opposite Try walking to Morte Point (pictured here) from Bull Point

Clockwise from top left See North Devon from the air – Fly Like A Bird offers tandem flights for novices; watch the sun set over Lundy Island; a surfer on Woolacombe beach

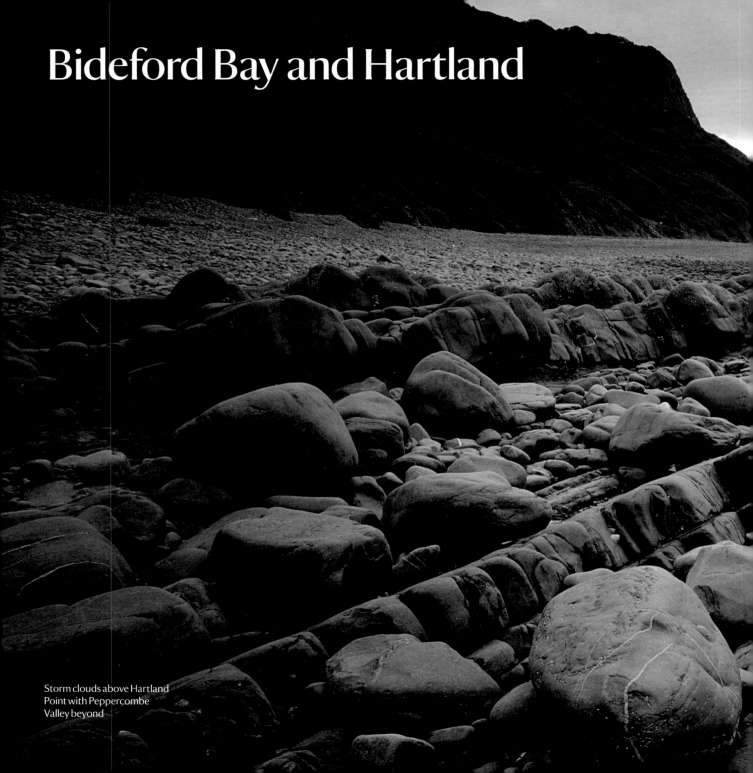

Bideford Bay and Hartland

Storm clouds above Hartland
Point with Peppercombe
Valley beyond

Bideford Bay Coast

This gentle, sheltered coastline, with its rounded cliffs cloaked in sessile oaks, isolated fishing villages nestled in deep wooded combes and streams rushing down valleys to form dramatic coastal waterfalls, is in marked contrast to the more exposed and rugged sections of North Devon's coastline. Here there's a real sense of peace and intimacy, heightened by the feeling of being cocooned in a woodland world with only brief glimpses of the sea and landscape beyond.

Westward Ho!

For a small coastal town Westward Ho! has an impressive number of claims to fame – most of them of a literary variety. It's the only place name in the UK with an exclamation mark. Its existence as a seaside resort – and its unusual name – is all down to the success of Charles Kingsley's swashbuckling historical tale *Westward Ho!*, published in 1855 and written in nearby Bideford during one of Kingsley's many stays in North Devon. The novel's fictional hero lived at Burrough Farm on the edge of Northam, which was given to the National Trust by Northam Council in 1967. The town is also the setting of Rudyard Kipling's book of short stories, *Stalky & Co* (1899), based on the author's schooldays at the local United Services College from 1878–81.

A gorse-covered hill to the west of Westward Ho!, where Kipling's characters smoked pipes and read books, was given to the National Trust in 1938 by the Kipling Memorial Fund and renamed Kipling Tors. The path up the hill passes an old coastguard lookout hut, built in 1911 following the tragic loss of 26 lives in the sinking of the *Thistlemoor* in 1909. The stone hut was restored by the Trust in 2009 and offers sweeping views of Bideford Bay, with a toposcope highlighting key features in the expansive seascape. Running along the coast below Kipling Tors is the scar of the short-lived Bideford–Westward Ho! to Appledore railway line (1901–17), which today forms part of the South West Coast Path.

The red cliffs

The distinctive red cliffs running between Peppercombe and Portledge are a prominent feature along this stretch of coastline. These outcrops from the Permian period (c.250–290 million years ago) are unique to the North Devon coast and were created when 'red beds' of mud and sandstone were deposited on top of older beds of folded Upper Carboniferous rock, creating what geologists refer to as unconformity between the two rock beds. For a fine view of these low, rounded red cliffs head to the remote pebbly beach at Peppercombe, accessed via a steep path once used by mules and carts laden with quicklime gathered from the beach lime kiln. Visit as the sun is setting across the bay and the cliffs appear to glow bright red.

Peppercombe Castle

High up the wooded slopes overlooking the beach are the earthwork remains of Peppercombe Castle, an Iron Age promontory fort and later the site of an elaborate Victorian castellated house, complete with formal gardens and a tennis court, built in the 1830s but abandoned following a landslide in 1909; its ruins are hidden beneath the undergrowth. Perched below the site is an eye-catching wooden bungalow, Castle Bungalow – a legacy of the Pine-Coffin family, who , in the 1920s, transferred this 'flat-pack' building in sections by horse and cart from London.

The orchards

Bideford Bay's sheltered coastline and mild climate provide an excellent environment for fruit trees to grow, with established orchards in Brownsham, Dunsland, East Titchberry and Peppercombe. In 2016 the National Trust uncovered an historical orchard in Peppercombe Valley – visible in postcards from the Victorian era and hidden for over 150 years under scrub – revealing three surviving fruit trees.

Above left The view from the remains of Peppercombe Castle

Above right The 1899 cover for *Westward Ho!* by Charles Kingsley

Portledge Estate

Owned by the Pine-Coffin family for almost 900 years, a proportion of the 308-hectare (777-acre) Portledge Estate was bought by the National Trust in 1988. Sheltered from prevailing south-westerlies by Hartland Peninsula and regularly engulfed by sea mists, this stretch of coastline enjoys a microclimate that sees ferns, mosses and lichens thrive in ancient woodlands. Two sessile oak-dominated woodlands, Worthygate Wood and Sloo Wood (both Sites of Special Scientific Interest), sandwiched between Peppercombe Valley and the isolated fishing village of Bucks Mills, are home to an array of nationally important lichens, including four rare species of Western Atlantic 'old woodland' lichen.

Bucks Mills

Along a coastline with numerous unreachable shorelines, the old fishing village of Bucks Mills is easily accessible by car, or on foot along the South West Coast Path, and is well worth a visit.

The village itself is historic and picturesque, while the narrow rocky beach is a haven for shore wildlife with plenty of rock pools teeming with life.

The Braunds

During the 19th century if your surname wasn't Braund, or you were not related to the Braund family, chances are you wouldn't have been warmly welcomed into Bucks Mills. At the time the hamlet was a Braund stronghold and the dark-haired and dark-eyed clan was notoriously intolerant of strangers. The 'King of Bucks' was Captain James Braund (1809–98), whose home, King's Cottage, still stands at the bottom of the small village.

What's in a name?

Following coastal erosion, the Old Mill is the last of the village's many corn mills that gave the village part of its name and were all powered by the local stream – its output seen today cascading over the cliffs as a waterfall onto the pebbly beach below. The origin of the word 'Bucks' is derived from the Saxon term for a homestead, *Buccas Htwise*.

Local industries

Herring fishing and lime burning – along with lawless activities associated with isolated coastal communities – were the main livelihoods of villagers during the 18th and 19th centuries. But with no harbour, along with a rocky foreshore and pebbly beach, it wasn't an easy task launching and unloading vessels. A quay was built in the late 16th century by Lord of the Manor of Bucks, Richard Cole – reputedly Old King Cole from the nursery rhyme and, according to legend, killed fighting pirates near Bucks Mills in 1615 – but over time it was swept away by the sea.

The remains of two lime kilns – one an unusually large square kiln that was aided by a horse-drawn winch that transported the burnt lime up an inclined plane to the village – are positioned above the beach. And at low tide a channel, called the Gut, is visible, which was arduously cut into the rocky foreshore to allow larger boats to unload their wares of limestone and coal brought over from South Wales.

A special boat

Unique to Bucks Mills were 12-foot (3.5-metre) long carvel-built fishing vessels, called Bucks Ledge boats, which allowed fishermen to launch over the large pebbles on the beach without causing any undue damage.

Take in the view

From the beach the coastal view westward takes in the picturesque fishing village of Clovelly (privately owned by the Hamlyn family since 1738), set into a steep, densely wooded combe with a river of white-washed cottages tumbling down to its small harbour, and the distinctive triangular sea arch of Blackchurch Rock in the distance. Closer to Bucks Mills a pebble bank called the Gore juts out from the foreshore; locally it's known as 'Devil's Causeway', following the legend that the Devil started building a route to Lundy Island, but progress was halted when

the Devil's shovel broke. This isn't Bucks Mills' only association with Lundy. The island regularly supplied grain for the village's corn mills, while fluctuating herring shoals in the mid-19th century lead villagers to work in Lundy's granite quarries, a grueling 17-mile (27km) boat trip across open sea.

The artists' studio

Bucks Mills' hidden gem is an artists' studio perched next to the beach slipway, of which the National Trust became custodian in 2008. From the outside it's an inconspicuous stone building with a green door. But step inside and you feel like you've been transported back in time – and in many ways you have. For 50 years the studio was the summer residence of artists Judith Ackland and Mary Stella Edwards, known for their evocative paintings of the North Devon landscape, but following Ackland's death in 1971 the studio door remained shut, leaving all the contents undisturbed. Today 'The Cabin' has been preserved almost exactly as the artists left it over 40 years ago, complete with books, paints and bric-a-brac. Throughout the year the National Trust runs open days for a rare opportunity to take a peek inside this timeless artists' retreat.

Above Visitors enjoying the sea air on Bucks Mills beach

Below left Captain James Braund, the 'King of Bucks'

Far left 'The Cabin', the former summer residence of artists Judith Ackland and Mary Stella Edwards

Hartland
North Coast

Tucked away in a little-known corner of Devon, the north-facing section of the Hartland Peninsula is one of North Devon's least visited areas.

But what the peninsula lacks in visitors it more than makes up for with dramatic, unspoilt stretches of coastline with fascinating geology, rare habitats and ancient farmland.

Brownsham

The isolated hamlet of Brownsham was donated to the National Trust in 1969 along with 124 hectares (307 acres) of surrounding woods and farmland that includes the largest area of Culm Grassland owned by the Trust (see p. 64). It has been standing for almost five centuries; records indicate there were tenants in Lower Brownsham farm as far back as 1521.

Another farm, the Grade II-listed Higher Brownsham, was built in the early 17th century for the Nicholl family, farmers and key players in the local glove-making industry. It features an intricately decorated plaster barrel ceiling in one of the bedrooms; over the centuries this has dropped and bulged, but restoration work carried out by the National Trust in 1989 means this surprise attraction to the modest farmhouse can still be seen (though by appointment only).

Right A view of Shipload Bay

Top right Bluebells in Beckland Wood

Beckland Wood

The mixed woodland habitat of Beckland Wood fills the land between Brownsham and the exposed cliff-top farmland and bracken-covered cliffs of Beckland Cliffs, which were acquired by the National Trust in 1976. At the highest point of Beckland Cliffs, 465 feet (142m) above sea level, lie the remains of Windbury Head Camp, an Iron Age hill fort and designated Scheduled Monument. Nearby stands a memorial to the crew of a Wellington bomber that crashed into the cliffs in thick sea mist on 13 April 1942.

From Windbury Head there's a spectacular panoramic view across Bideford Bay: to your east the secluded cove of old smugglers' haunt Mouth Mill and the distinctive triangular stack of Blackchurch Rock, with its two 'windows' cut by sea erosion; beyond this the long golden-sand beach of Saunton Sands – backed by the UNESCO Biosphere Reserve of Braunton Burrows – featuring the bright white oblong of Saunton Sands Hotel set into the cliffs; and finally sweeping westward to take in the headlands of Baggy Point and Morte Point and, on a clear day, the distant Exmoor hills.

East Titchberry

It doesn't take much to imagine the picturesque buildings of East Titchberry Farm as a hive of activity over 500 years ago. The remote medieval farmstead, just east of Hartland Point, was given to the National Trust by Miss Abraham in 1943, along with 64 hectares (158 acres) of cliff-top farmland. The oldest building is the 15th-century thatched farmhouse, while the cob-and-thatch granary, with its external dove holes under the eaves, was built in the late 17th to early 18th century.

Across a track from the farmyard you'll find a former malthouse, built at around the same time as the granary. This used locally grown barley, cultivated on the unusually dry coastal farmland surrounding the farm (resulting in the name of a

nearby cove, Barley Bay) to produce malt for making beer. The building was later used as a ciderhouse.

Shipload Bay

A short walk from the car-park at East Titchberry brings you to the aptly named Shipload Bay. In years gone by, smugglers would have unloaded contraband from vessels here before transporting it to nearby caves. Landslides have since demolished the mule track used by smugglers, as well as the wooden steps built by the National Trust in 1981, making the beach inaccessible, except by boat or kayak. But this means grey seals have claimed it as their own and can often be seen from the cliff-top bathing on the sandy beach, while peregrine falcons, kestrels and fulmars breed on the steeply sloping cliffs surrounding the bay.

Along the east side of the bay impressive rock formations are exposed, the result of intense folding and faulting in the sandstone and shale rock millions of years ago. Standing prominently on the cliff edge west of Shipload Bay is the large white Civil Aviation Authority radar dome – a distinctive landmark visible from as far away as Baggy Point and Lundy Island – located on the site of the original Second World War RAF radar station, which closed in 1987.

Hartland Atlantic Coast and Dunsland

The moment you turn left at Hartland Point to join the west-facing Atlantic coast, the scenery changes dramatically. Gone are the gentle sheltered combes and soft wooded cliffs, replaced by an exposed and rugged coastline of high jagged cliffs and crashing waves. It's desolate, wild and stunningly beautiful.

Welcombe Mouth

In 2008 the National Trust acquired the secluded beach of Welcombe Mouth. At low tide, its wave-cut platform is teeming with rock pools alive with seashore species waiting to be discovered. The beach is a designated SSSI and a Geological Conservation Review Site for its spectacular and highly visible geological features – the dramatic rock folds in the cliffs can be seen near to where an impressive waterfall spills off the cliffs onto the beach.

Music fans may also be interested to learn that in December 1970 the rock band Deep Purple recorded tracks for their album *Fireball* (released the following year) at The Hermitage, the large white house nestled in the valley overlooking Welcombe Mouth.

Embury Beacon

The steep cliffs and agricultural coastland north of Welcombe Mouth, as far as South Hole Farm, were acquired by the National Trust in 1996 and take in the remains of an Iron Age hill fort, Embury Beacon – over two thirds now lost to coastal erosion. Excavations of the site in the 1970s unearthed artifacts dating to 200BC. From its elevation at 510 feet (155m) above sea level you're greeted with spectacular views south along the North Cornish coast to distant Trevose Head, and north to the less familiar, shorter edge of Lundy Island.

Left A view of Welcombe Mouth

The Iron Coast

With a long list of ships having been wrecked here, it's no surprise that the Hartland Atlantic Coast is known as the 'Iron Coast'. The rusting remains of many vessels lie on the seabed between Welcombe Mouth and Embury Beacon.

Dunsland: the lost country estate

The ancient parkland at Dunsland, near Holsworthy, is a remote and tranquil place to visit. But while exploring its vast woodland pastures and designed landscape it's difficult to ignore the ghostly sense of the grand house that once stood in its midst.

On a meadow of grassland, which today invites you to roll out a blanket and enjoy a picnic overlooking the parkland, once stood Dunsland House, a Grade I-listed building of Tudor origin. Since the days of William the Conqueror the house, which was enlarged in the 17th century, had descended by inheritance through seven families, before it was bought by two separate owners (in 1945 and 1950) and finally, with the house in a state of decay, by the National Trust in 1954. With the help of grants the neglected house underwent extensive restoration and gradually returned to its former glory as a stately home.

Then, in the early hours of 18 November 1967 – weeks before Dunsland House was due to open to the public – a fire swept through the building. Within a few hours the house was reduced to a smoking ruin. Thankfully the live-in caretakers escaped unharmed, but the fire devastated the

whole building, along with destroying all its contents (including many items on loan from private owners), leaving no option but to bulldoze the blackened shell to the ground. Today very little remains of the original Dunsland Estate, except a stone lintel from the house and two gate-posts, along with a coach house, stable block and walled garden, a sad end to over 900 years of history.

The woodlands

Fifty years later, the 37 hectares (92 acres) of woodland pasture surrounding the site of Dunsland House have been transformed into a haven for wildlife, with the area granted SSSI status for its lichen communities and deadwood invertebrates. The parkland is home to a large variety of trees, including 700-year-old sweet chestnuts, and in spring the woodland floor is covered in bluebells, primroses and celandines. A new orchard – established by the National Trust in 2002 – has been planted with 75 fruit trees, including 14 local varieties of plums, pears and apples. Resident bees help bring Dunsland's orchards and flower meadows to life.

Above A path through the Dunsland estate

Below Dunsland Manor prior to the devastating fire

Things to see and do at Bideford Bay and Hartland

Walk Bucks Mills to Peppercombe

Follow a 5.5-mile (8.8km) circular walk through ancient woodlands teeming with birds, plants and rare lichen. The walk takes you along a high coastal section of the South West Coast Path, with glimpses of the sea through the sessile oak trees, before dropping into the densely wooded Peppercombe Valley where a brief diversion to a remote pebbly beach offers a fine view of the area's distinctive red cliffs.

Go on a wildlife cruise

During the summer months the National Trust runs sunset wildlife cruises from the fishing village of Clovelly. As the sun sets over Lundy Island you can enjoy a magical evening voyage along the North Devon coast in the company of a knowledgeable Trust ranger, with excellent opportunities to see seabirds, marine life and stunning coastal scenery.

Picnic at Peace Park

With its well-positioned benches and spectacular sea views, Mount Pleasant (known locally as Peace Park), a small tree-lined park on the western edge of Clovelly, is an excellent picnic spot. It was given to the National Trust in 1921 by Mrs Christine Hamlyn, the then owner of the Clovelly estate, in memory of the local men who died in the First World War.

Follow a nature trail

On set days, for example some days during school holidays, you can pick up a free trail map from the National Trust car-park at Brownsham and follow a gentle family friendly nature trail in search of the hidden animal clues through the beautiful Beckland Woods. The woods are home to damp-loving plants and a variety of woodland birds, and in spring the slopes are a haze of bluebells and the air full of bird song.

Right Discover the distinctive red rock at Peppercombe's pebble beach as part of a circular walk from Bucks Mills

Below left Enjoy a peaceful stroll through the wooded Peppercombe Valley

Below right Peppercombe Bothy offers basic accommodation with extraordinary views

Try a running trail

Why not try picking up the pace while enjoying some spectacular coastal views. For anybody wanting to try trail running the National Trust has created circular run routes from National Trust car-parks. There is a one-mile (1.6km) circular run at Welcombe Mouth, a two-mile (3.2km) circular run at Brownsham and a three-mile (4.8km) circular run at East Titchberry.

Explore Burough Farm

Follow a gentle 1.25-mile (2km) circular walk that takes you across farmland, through woodland and along the River Torridge, where at low tide you can spot the sand-filled remains of four Victorian sailing ships. The National Trust was given this agricultural land on the edge of Northam in 1967; today it stands out as a green oasis nestled between built-up residential areas.

Stay in Peppercombe Bothy

Nestled in Peppercombe Valley, this secluded stone building is a perfect hideaway for those looking to enjoy the simplicity of life in the outdoors. The basic accommodation sleeps up to four people and is certainly a contender for the best view from a loo – a glorious, uninterrupted seascape across Bideford Bay.

Camp at Brownsham

Snuggle up underneath the thatched roof of a replica Iron Age hut, or pitch your tent in an enclosed grassland area for your chance to wake up in the great outdoors. The site offers campers a composting toilet, running water, a fire pit and an outdoor oven, as well as a peaceful and wild location on the remote Hartland Peninsula. The National Trust campsite is available in the summer months on a first-come, first-served basis.

Extending Your Stay

From relaxing holidays in unusual cottages to helping the Trust out around the area, there are lots of ways to extend your holiday in North Devon.

Accommodation

Whether you prefer staying in a manor house or pitching your tent in a remote camping spot, the National Trust offers a variety of interesting and unique accommodation options in North Devon.

Holiday cottages

In West Exmoor you can stay in a Lighthouse Keeper's Cottage (sleeps 10) perched on the edge of Foreland Point in splendid isolation, or opt for West Challacombe Manor (sleeps five), a 15th-century manor with a stunning hammer-beam ceiling (see p. 19). You may prefer Countisbury Hill Cottage (sleeps four), a cosy cottage opposite a pub, or Combe Park Lodge (sleeps four) located deep in the wooded East Lyn Valley and an ideal base for walkers. Within a private gated area in Peppercombe Valley there's the option to stay in one of three quaint Coastguard Cottages (sleeps two to four) or the charming Combe Cottage (sleeps four) – they are all within easy reach of a remote pebbly beach and leave you feeling like you're miles from anywhere.

Back to basics

For a real taste of back-to-basics outdoor living you can't beat a bothy or a spot of camping. Bothies are basic shelters in converted old buildings with no heating, electricity or shower facilities – imagine camping with a solid roof. The National Trust bothies at Foreland, Heddon Orchard and Peppercombe have basic toilet facilities, running water and raised sleeping platforms, but above all they are located in unique locations and are the perfect way to get close to nature. All sleep up to four humans and two dogs.

During July and August you can pitch your tent at two designated camping sites, at Heddon Valley and Brownsham. Both are quiet, isolated sites set up with a composting toilet, running water and a fire pit.

Useful links
Accommodation: nationaltrust.org.uk/
holidays | 0344 800 2070
Volunteering: nationaltrust.org.uk/
volunteer, or email northdevon@
nationaltrust.org.uk to register interest
Working holidays: nationaltrust.org.uk/
holidays/working-holidays

Opposite Volunteers on working holidays might stay in the Exmoor Basecamp

Above Tucked away in woodland near Bideford, these 18th-century, terraced 'cob cottages' originally housed officers of the Preventive Service, who prevented smuggling – later the Coastguard Service. They are now known as 'Coastguard Cottages' and can be rented as holiday accommodation

Above right The lighthouse at Lighthouse Keeper's Cottage still functions today (though the foghorn is no longer). Sleeping 10, it's perfect for large groups looking for a dramatic, unusual place to stay

For large groups, great value options are the Exmoor Bunkhouse (sleeps 18) or Butter Hill Barn (sleeps six), both located in Countisbury, an ideal spot for exploring Exmoor. They have bunk-bed dormitories, hot showers and fully equipped kitchens.

Volunteering

Volunteering with the National Trust is an exciting and sociable way to learn new skills, work in spectacular settings and lend a hand to a great cause. There are plenty of volunteering opportunities available in North Devon, such as car-park assistants at Baggy Point, wildlife monitors, office administrators, event photographers, and helping rangers with ongoing conservation tasks – as the saying goes 'many hands make light work'.

Working Holidays

Each year the National Trust hosts a number of working holidays in North Devon, where participants can enjoy unique experiences in stunning coastal locations while working alongside and learning new skills from experts.

Staying at the Exmoor Bunkhouse, these week-long active holidays involve helping rangers with traditional conservation tasks, such as restoring dry-stone walls, tackling invasive species, maintaining coastal footpaths, cleaning beaches or undertaking sand dune management. You might also be able to try your hand at local outdoor activities, including coasteering, trail running, climbing, sea kayaking and surfing. Along with enjoying an active holiday in the great outdoors, you will also have the satisfaction of helping to keep North Devon looking its best.

Looking after North Devon

In North Devon the National Trust cares for over 3,200 hectares (8,000 acres) of land, 50 miles of coastline and 101 miles of footpath in a diverse landscape that includes woods, moors, beaches, farmland and meadows.

Above Volunteers help to repair a wall

Above right The burnet moth has been allowed to thrive due to the Trust's coastal and heathland management programme and 'swaling'

Below right Willow leaf beetles are just one of the species that have been able to thrive thanks to the Trust's careful habitat management

It's a challenging task but a responsibility that we take seriously. Our rangers, staff and volunteers work all-year-round to protect North Devon's coast and countryside so that it can be enjoyed by future generations.

Coastal erosion

Most of the National Trust-owned coastline lies in the nationally protected catchment of the North Devon Coast AONB and it's this natural beauty that attracts thousands of visitors to the region every year. But the constant footfall comes at a price: coastal erosion. The Trust spends a lot of time maintaining many miles of coastal and inland footpaths and employing methods to reduce the impact of coastal erosion by humans, as well as from environmental factors such as winter storms and tidal surges.

One of the Trust's biggest tasks, undertaken by a team of volunteers, is the annual construction of a half-mile-long (0.8km) wooden fence along the front edge of the sand dunes at Woolacombe beach (in place between May and October). The fence has been used for over 30 years and protects the vulnerable dune system from severe trampling in the height of the summer.

Woodland management

The swathes of ancient oak woodland that cloak the cliffs and combes of West Exmoor and Bideford Bay are a reminder of a time when oak was the main timber product in the UK. Following years of established management practices, by the end of the First World War these broadleaved woodlands were abandoned, leaving acres of neglected ancient woodland dominated by sessile oak trees. This species lets in little light through its dense canopy, impacting on habitats in the lower canopies. Since taking ownership of these woodlands, the National Trust has restored traditional woodland management methods, such as coppicing (cutting down young tree stems to near ground level) and pollarding (removing the top of the tree above browsing

beech trees. Over the past decade the Trust has carried out a continual eradication programme that involves injecting tiny amounts of weed killer into the plant's stems to kill off the invasive plants and allow other species to thrive.

Coastal heathland

The National Trust owns the majority of the coastal heathland in North Devon, a scarce and declining habitat that has fallen victim to intensive farming and poor management over the past 200 years. The extensive areas of coastal heathland managed by the Trust all fall within designated SSSI for their diverse range of habitats that support rare plants, invertebrates and breeding birds. But these heathland areas require careful and constant management, in particular Exmoor's high coastal heaths at Trentishoe and Countisbury. Along with the importance of grazing by sheep, cows and Exmoor ponies, every year in late winter the National Trust carries out the traditional practice of swaling, where small areas of heath are deliberately burnt to control the growth of gorse and to encourage the regeneration of heather – the new growth allows insect life to thrive, including rare weevils, leaf beetles and burnet moths.

Historical preservation

The Trust is fortunate to have seven Iron Age hill forts on its land, and part of its work is helping to preserve these. By regularly cutting back any encroaching bracken, we ensure that roots do not damage any precious archaeological features.

With some of the dry-stone walls and stone-faced hedge-banks around Woolacombe dating back almost 200 years they form an important part of the area's heritage, as well as providing homes to wildlife such as bank voles, frogs and slow worms. It costs the Trust £100 to repair just one metre of wall, but their historical and natural significance means it's money well spent.

height) to create sustainable woods of mixed age groups and species (many native) that support a diversity of flora and fauna, including rich communities of lichens and wildflowers, as well as populations of dormice.

The spread of non-native species such as rhododendron is an ongoing conservation project. Although its flowers look pretty, the negative impact this fast-growing and highly invasive species has on a site far outweigh its attributes – not only is it poisonous to wildlife, but it also carries diseases that spread to oak and

Looking after the countryside: case studies

West Exmoor: Heddon Valley – the high brown fritillary

Heddon Valley is home to a large variety of butterflies that can be seen flying around its sunny bracken-covered slopes between June and early August. But it's the increase in the population of the high brown fritillary – the UK's most endangered butterfly – that has been a conservation success story for the National Trust.

This large, fast-flying butterfly with bright orange and black wings was once widespread in the UK, but since the 1950s its numbers have declined dramatically due to changes in land management impacting on its breeding habitat. Today, Heddon Valley is one of only four sites in the country where the high brown fritillary thrives thanks to the Trust's careful habitat maintenance.

Over the past decade the Trust has focused on clearing scrub and tramping down bracken that shades the growth of common dog-violet, the main foodplant for the high brown fritillary larvae. On Heddon Valley's steep slopes, where grazing by cattle and ponies is not feasible, teams of volunteers manually create runnels (paths) through the bracken using planks of wood, mimicking the effects of grazing animals. By creating a network of runnels the adult butterflies are able to get underneath the bracken to lay their eggs on dead bracken litter or dog-violet leaves.

In 2016 a survey by Butterfly Conservation reported a 646 per cent increase in the population of high brown fritillaries in Exmoor over a 14-year period, with recent sightings of the species in two new sites in Heddon Valley. As well as the high brown fritillary, the National Trust's habitat management also supports a number of other butterflies, including the silver-washed fritillary – frequently seen in July and August – the small pearl-bordered fritillary and the dark green fritillary.

Croyde, Woolacombe and Ilfracombe: Woolacombe Warren – dune cattle grazing

A herd of large red cows grazing on scrub is perhaps not what you would expect to stumble upon while walking through sand dunes. But during the winter months this is exactly what you'll find at Woolacombe Warren as part of a conservation project run by the National Trust in partnership with a local tenant farmer and their herd of North Devon Red cattle.

Historically the National Trust has managed this vast dune habitat using either machinery or manpower to cut back or rake out the invasive scrub, which shades out important dune plant species that support a rich variety of wildlife. Introducing a small herd of cows to graze the dunes creates a range of scrub height that encourages the growth of a wider range of wildflowers.

During the winter of 2016, 10 North Devon Reds grazed six hectares (15 acres) of dune habitat at the southern end of the Warren.

Not wanting to ruin the landscape with gates, stiles and fencing – and inhibit public access to Woolacombe Warren – an innovative system called 'invisible fencing' was implemented, which saw the cows fitted with collars that responded to radio signals emitted by a cable buried around the designated grazing area. If the cows strayed near the cable an audio sound was activated. If they moved any closer, they received a small electrical pulse from the collar. However, it didn't take long for the cows to learn the system and they rarely tested the boundaries.

The success of the trial project has been two fold. For the female cows they spent winter outdoors grazing on fresh roughage, which was good for their diet and prepared them for the breeding season. As for the dune habitat, the benefit became abundantly clear as the season progressed, with better-than-expected displays of primroses and bluebells and an increase in the variety of wildflower populations, including bird's-foot trefoil and pyramidal orchids, as well as the return of bee orchids to the dunes.

Opposite A male high brown fritillary butterfly at Heddon Valley; the species' population has increased significantly in Exmoor in recent years

Above The North Devon Reds that help graze Woolacombe Warren and manage the habitat there

Case studies (continued)

Bideford Bay and Hartland: Brownsham Moors – Culm grassland

It's easy to overlook the marshy pasture, wet heath and scrubby woodland that make up Brownsham Moors, but despite its lack of immediate appeal this unassuming patch of Culm grassland – a term given to damp, unimproved grasslands that have developed above a geological strata, known as the Culm Measures – is a unique and internationally threatened habitat.

The National Trust has carefully managed Brownsham Moors – the largest area of Culm grassland owned by the Trust – since 1998. During this time the Trust has cleared 12 hectares (29 acres) of scrub and young woodland to allow the Culm grassland to regenerate. Key plant species soon established themselves, including the nationally scarce wavy St John's wort and yellow bartsia, as well as a diversity of butterflies, moths, dragonflies and invertebrates. Damp grassland is an important habitat for the threatened marsh fritillary butterfly, whose main foodplant, devil's bit scabious, is found in abundance at Brownsham Moors.

The Culm grassland on Brownsham Moors requires constant and careful management by the National Trust. The main focus is the ongoing task of keeping on top of scrub regrowth, but as a wet area of land this isn't always an easy task. Along with mechanical methods and the traditional method of swaling (controlled burning), the area is also grazed by Highland cattle provided by a tenant farmer – all these

techniques create a varied age structure to the vegetation and encourage a rich diversity of wildlife species.

Without the Trust's intervention, Brownsham Moors' Culm grassland would have, over the past 20 years, been lost beneath overgrown scrub and woodland – a reality that occurred throughout the Culm landscape of North Devon and North East Cornwall (the only areas this habitat is found) during the 1980s when modern farming and lack of management led to the loss of almost 50 per cent of the habitat. Although Brownsham Moors is only a small segment of the wider Culm landscape, its regeneration as a thriving patch of Culm grassland is a positive step forward for this rare habitat.

Above St John's Wort (left) and yellow bartsia (right) are just some of the species establishing themselves on Brownsham Moors